Displaced Dolls and Oviducts

poems by

Marigo J. Stathis

Finishing Line Press
Georgetown, Kentucky

Displaced Dolls and Oviducts

To Warren, who summoned my mettle
To Abby and Lucy, who demonstrate what it means
to shine from within

ACKNOWLEDGMENTS

My utmost gratitude is extended to the editors of publications in which some of these poems appeared or are forthcoming:

34th Parallel Magazine: "Timebombing"
The Baltimore City Paper: "The Ladies' Room"; "Transformation"
The Baltimore Sun: "The Ladies' Room"
Bear Creek Haiku: "Inclemency"
Facedown: "At the Stake"; "Freeze-frames: Brother's Haikus"; "The Ladies' Room"; "One of our Best Kept Secrets"; "Toaster"
FanStory: "Invasion"
Lite Journal of Satire and Creativity: "Best Friends Meeting in the Heart of New York City"; "Mimi"; "Not Just Another Thanksgiving Day"
The Loch Raven Review: "Narcissus and Echo"
Minerva Rising Press, The Keeping Room: "A Year to Heal"
The National Library of Poetry: "Laundromat"

Publisher: Leah Huete de Maines
Editor: Christen Kincaid
Cover Art: Marigo J. Stathis
Author Photo: Marigo J. Stathis
Cover Design: Elizabeth Maines McCleavy

Order online: www.finishinglinepress.com
also available on amazon.com

Author inquiries and mail orders:
Finishing Line Press
PO Box 1626
Georgetown, Kentucky 40324
USA

Table of Contents

Invasion

The poet's craft lands!

Her alien,
scratch-and-sniff
words
threaten
book infested,
dead ideas
bred and
read by
the misinformed
and misled.

Toaster

I am like you, toaster:
      metal-bruised mirror of
            fingerprints and timedusts,
       slotted cube of outshiny smiles,
              burning veils of secrets still inward,
              crusted, smoked suicide.

Once crumb-spilled,
       will our coils more readily welcome the heat?

Will we resist the temptation or succumb
       to once more brand marks on any bread,
each breakfasted day's worth of fresh offerings?

You will remember this fuseblown jolt.
       We are one and the same, toaster:
             appliances, and nothing more.

The Ladies' Room

There's a stranger in the stall in front of me.
      Ignoring the room's smell,
she memorizes the words,
      absorbs the messages.
She touches the wall,
      as if the scribbles could change her.

Her magic marker squeaks,
      pours forth its juice,
the advice and fear
      of a woman who feels compelled to leave her mark.

These are the hieroglyphics of sisterhood,
      images the janitor's sweat
will never scrub away.
      Even the occasional, *"For a good time, call..."*
has a spirit that can't be broken by S.O.S.

As I wait for my turn,
      I know in a moment,
this stranger will emerge
      to warm palm-skin with paper-towel embrace,
seeking, once more, the mirror's guidance,
      as if the lines on her face could tell her something
she doesn't already know.

Reunion

On the fortnight of spring,
at half past eleven,
Arcadia burst
to usher in
flush of gushing
spirits immersed,
uncoiled laughter,
long-lost girlfriends,
newly embraced,
as well-lit slivers.

Those photons,
that bleed within
exposed us for
who we really are:

labyrinths,
planes,
obtuse angles,
inverting,
turning,
forever
folding,
pulsing
things of beauty,
with contused cores—

injured fragments,
human origami.

Transformation

Tattoo girl,
your ink unfurls
micropointed purpose.

With skins as slates,
how do you rate
the reasons all have come here?

On petalscripts and dragonwings,
curves of many branding things,
you bleed the past right from them.

If from tearsquinted eyes,
they witness warm running dyes,
what fainting could progress, then?

But, it's not the art
of flawless skulls and hearts
that renders them more composed.

In contrast to life's blows,
unexpectedly thrown,
it's the choosing of their own scars.

Garden of the Gods

Motorcycle bound,
we weave figure eights
on this dusty road,
towards red-gilded grove.

The pronghorns know
this is just another tour of turns
for you, as I spin within,
heady by laughter's pulse and
the way your sweaty shoulder
baptizes my chin,
desert butterflies in abdomen.

I gasp in arches and spikes,
as wise, russet mother watches,
offering to our still-parched hearts
more sap of aspen.

Ever rugged, solitary and present,
I understand my kind,
hungry magpie,
surveying the scene,
searching for signs
in any shiny thing:
        half-moon of smile,
        sole slab of skin,
        oasis for the ravenous—
I drink it all in.

As we pass kissing camels' cathedral spires,
I think in another life I may have been yours,
naked shaman of the white-throated swift,
who dwelled among bison and elk,
beseeching epochal help
from the bighorn and fox.

But today, among these blushing rocks,
we are mere tiger beetles or honey ants
the canyon wren keeps in view,
while voyeur of venom and blue,
with eyes of obsidian,
rattles our tale and swallows
any chance for something else
beneath the shade of cottonwoods.

A Year to Heal

I once woke up
in wild winter,
paralyzed by change,
when claws emerged
and storms surged
sunken snow and
white wombs
from where I came.

In mere months,
seduced by scents,
spanned by veins,
I unfolded into sun,
blossomed in rain
with vernal wings—
a quivering,
unconfident display.

Then the splash—
summer's solstice,
and dash of depths,
when I submerged,
floundering and
cursed to accept
annulled remorse,
until lungs
surfaced again.

By the time
it was autumn,
seasoned and ready,
I left it all behind—
the glacier and blue
icy truth of you:
striated river of tears,
slow-moving
misogynist,
seeker of the shear
story that never ends.

In just a year,
I found strength beyond
the fossil fixed in granite,
once living: our memory.

Best Friends, Meeting in the Heart of New York City

It took three hours' worth of Amtrakking to reach that dragon,
        that sweats and spits fire from a million mouths,
        shining yellow wrath
from a thousand sons of a thousand taxicabbed sons.
        That weekend, though, the dragon would not win.

Powerful with mutual admiration,
        we could have become each other's armor,
but chose instead to be exposed.

Hugging and clinging like marsupials,
        we giggled, double-aliced in that fallen wonderland.
We expanded and overflowed like the Hudson after rain,
        and our laughter, the rain,
spilled so hard and heavy,
        our umbrella sagged beneath the weight,
couldn't cover us, fat with ego.

Together, we were walking hieroglyphics,
        enigmatic girls carving our presence on each sidewalk,
        no one able to decode us,
voicing words of a hidden tongue only we knew,
        sounds sticking to our skins, like crazy glue.

Vendors' falafels and croissants,
        complete with magic grease,
gave us the strength to shield ourselves
        from the day's worth of city fleas,
as we continued in our relentless quest
        to find the ultimate henna and cologne,
excaliburs of Spanish Harlem street sales.

By nightfall, Ki-Mang's jests and the white chocolate mousse
of Broadway and 81st tempted us to nearly drop swords of jest,
but it was Lucy's Blue Whales that saved us,
        Medusa and Jezebel,
until we brought that dragon to its knees
        and held up our drinks, flags of victory.

Beyond the moat,
        not too much later,
we were safe in your dorm-room.
Cigarette butts burned until dawn and
        before sleep stole,
we shared ever larger rings of smoked secrets
        a celebrational rite that said:
Nothing could touch us two soulful warriors,
        best friends,
so full of ourselves.

Emergence

In 2020- 2021, the CDC reported U.S. adults experienced adverse mental health conditions associated with COVID-19. Younger adults were among those who reported having experienced disproportionately worse mental health outcomes, increased substance use, and elevated suicidal ideation.

Someone should have checked on Blythe
long before Brood X arrived,
long before the police were called,
and death's certificate was signed.

The coroner said it was a natural end,
but there can be nothing normal
about a young girl's body spread in rigor
on sheets that expose cold epidermal.

The moment we heard the news
was just before we were slated to phone,
catch up, and invite her to our home.
Vaccinated, we felt it safe to condone.

We weren't savvy or street-smart enough
to suspect her loss of sobriety,
the truth of what she battled alone:
addiction, abandonment, anxiety.

Her parents were the bad kids she raised,
habitually emerging to grovel and crawl:
a quivering mother quoting scripture,
a daddy dropping drinks 'til dawn.

Today, the cicadas fly lopsided and
the air is many-wings-thick
with decibels of sincere mourning.

As we wait for our turn to be judged,
from viral plagues of ignorance:

> May we clink to toasts of "might have been"
> while begging pardon from guileless corpses.

> Let us dig deep holes to aerate soils,
> graves for our deceptive narratives.

Last Night in New Orleans

Last night,
             My head spun fast
         at the Absinthe,
                 a sunglassed-alligator
         smiled pointed teeth and laughed
                 as Mint Juleps tap-danced
         slippery, ice-cubed chatter
                 to battered guitar blues.

Last night,
                 a crawfish shined my shoes,
         then led me to Jackson Square,
                 where cornstalks dare to embrace
         morning glories on
                 19th-century balconies, iron-laced
         images;
                 there, I saw the buggy horses bicker, face to face,
         about who'd wear the loveliest straw-hat,
                 orchid-covered, and all
         that jazz.

Last night,
                 I had pizzazz.
         I walked down Decatur alleys of the voodoo queen.
                 God,
         what a scene:
                 pin-poking multiple Trump-doll busts,
         trading masks made of Mississippi River sun-dried dust.

Last night,
                 Hanging out at Preservation Hall made me lust
         to hear that gentle-rapping
                 of Eddie, the
         long-fingernailed tray tap-tapping
                 man.

Last night,
                 my early-to-bed plans
         gave in to the rhythm,
                 to the sway,
         everything in the air said it was time

                    to go to the swamp
        and accompany
                    white Cyprus on the copper-plated
        piano for the dancing—
                    mud's slip and slide.

Last night,
                    I took a sternwheel ride,
        winged high in the Louisiana sky,
                    while the moon played a sax
        that cast
                    down the spiciest Cajun-eclipse
        the Vieux-Carré ever saw.

Freeze-frames: Brother's Haikus

And this photo holds
       faded freeze frames, still moving,
our lives have time lapsed.

Beyond the laughter,
       frisbees freely spun frolic,
caught bold, brazen smiles.

The mushroom-cut boy,
       collecting insects in jars,
had feelers all his own.

Cocooned color changed
       mother's sting of ritual,
sister's crawl of love.

Knocks on minddoors, faint,
       scratches on softened skins, soiled,
shrewd games of Scrabble.

Pink bubbles, bursting,
       one blow consumed by others:
Contest of the young.

Hair tufts, brown in fall,
       assumed earth star's hues; the gold
healed us whole each June.

Lessons of languid
       summer moments left us bruised,
craving new mentors.

Red scooters rolling;
       our hills welcomed the import
of ripe kids' races.

Now, you run again,
       corporate rules unflinching;
Remember the wings.

Accidental

In the company of confidantes,
it wasn't wise to entertain spilled milk,
mishaps of distracted brats, bursting
from Hubba Bubba gum cracks and
burps of Dinty-Moore-Pop-Tart-Tang—
leftovers of divorce in the 70's.

Back then, the perfect home was designed of
retro fabrics ill-equipped to absorb
stains of single moms and their clumsy kids.

When gossip and menstruations were
interrupted by the accidental splash,
it was best to laugh just before
trashing dolls and slapping dreams.

Afterall, daughters needed to learn early
they wouldn't always return to
what was there when they left.

I remember seven:

the empty dollhouse,
displaced dresses and
miniature pleas of
broken Barbies in the bin,
echoes of arguments
they couldn't win.

My loving aunts were yard's trio of trees,
who opened teepee limb-arms,
offering cover during hours when
mother's brain cracked in half,
and the air pulsed like a scorned heart,
exchanging oxygen for screams.

In those days, they didn't call it by its real name.

Bruises came from natural falls,
and put-downs were imagined,
while hidden daddies waited for
widely-spaced weekends
and their visitation rights.

Not Just Another Thanksgiving Day

Mediterranean-stuffing stuck to mouth rooftops,
        while on lead crystal stages,
        yams squirmed with sweet potatoes
in the bouzouki dance of Thanksgiving Day.

The dinner hours flew by as we,
        horde of Greeks,
talked over one another,
        with conversations as debates,
the loudest winged words winning.

By dessert,
        we devolved into pavlovian dogs,
salivating for baklava
        catcalling *Polykala.*

Despite the murmurings,
        second helpings,
and debauchery,
        I noticed Pota uncomfortably poking at a turkey sliver.

Among the bounce and bacchanal,
        she stood out, all skin and bones,
a contrast to the summer before,
        when she carried her muscular frame
like a panther.

On this day of harvest and gratitude,
        she deflected questions about her weight,
focusing instead on the difficulty of freshman French
        and the lacrosse coach who made her run five miles a day.

As she spoke, I tasted sublayers of doubt and fear
        betrayed by stringy hair and protruding vertebrae.
I wondered what, if anything, I should do or say
        to convince her she was not alone,
on the female warrior's path to self-worth and discovery.

She needed different mental weapons;
        I wanted to tell her about the ones that worked for me;
but my hesitation cost,
        as she excused herself from the table and retreated,
the bathroom door's slam as her exclamation point.

Narcissus and Echo

Today, while passing fancy store window,
        she avoids the reflections and
frozen leers of jaunty mannequins
        with their flawless skin and smiles.
Instead, her gaze falls on sidewalk slabs
        and cracked concrete.

The thought of plastic and porcelain
        brings back memories of school reunions,
where a queen always claimed the fairest throne;
        in every crowd,
Hera pierces beauty with blue-green eyes,
        as Artemis vomits bile in the bathroom.

On this day,
        she defies traffic signals
and crosses streets without looking both ways, first,
        eager for
somewhere to call
        home.

As she boards the MTA and
        sits next to Juno, the sleeping bag lady,
she wonders
        why she was taught to speak last,
never first,
        never heard
or protected from curses,
        and why it's better to repeat what was already said.

She pays the price for humble strolls
        around a broken childhood and city;
By every pile of water,
        she waits to catch a glimpse of
might have been.

When she reaches her place,
        and finds the right key to open the space
she sees him smiling in the mirror,
        shaving a five o'clock shadow,
in love with himself,
        and, for the first time, speechless and muted,
she understands the importance of myth,
        the safety of cave.

Queen of the Highway

I got it from my Daddy,
        these genes of drive,
loving every ride,
        so long as a wheel's what I'm behind.

Every journey's a spice;
        amidst bland meals of nice days,
I lust for turbine, novel places,
        and wide-open spaces.

I'll be the first to admit,
        I have also inherited
the need to be queen,
        changing speed from ladylike to obscene.

Middle finger rising in two seconds or less,
        the best-of-the-best get pissed,
but I've a tough time letting it rest,
        my patience put to the test.

Every roadblock's an obstacle,
        each bottleneck a race;
I have traversed the finest,
        and I have set the pace.

From Canada to Kentucky,
        Moscow, Nassau, and Athens, too,
every highway I enter inevitably
        becomes vehicular zoo.

God bless the cops who have stopped me,
        before I committed the crime;
when I have somewhere to go,
        there's just no time for slow.

No pothole's too deep,
        no lane too gray,
to stop these pedal-metaled feet.
        Hey, Mr. Type A, I will brake your angry ass into the grass
the next time you tailgate THIS sass!

I'm not gonna lie,
        I can be road rage personified,
a break-the-sound-barrier-sort-of-beast:
        hear my 4-cylinder engine roar.

But don't blame me,
        once supercoiled DNA;
I'm now the unraveled fate
        of molecular biology.

Thank You, Father

Disciplined in the playground,
        in dress of lace and white gossamer,
I tried not to burn alabaster thighs on sliding board friction,
        promised to avoid sandbox holocaust,
while stretching to the last monkey bar,
        sweat neatly hidden,
while you waited in the background,
        one eyebrow raised.

I listened well,
        and always tried to make you proud
of being glass doll's protector.

Now, on sparkling Sundays,
        I am sometimes drawn to the parks
where the loud giants are,
        those who haven't yet discovered their power,
while bringing ebullience to grounds,
        where slippery feet
plod zigzag on gaping
        muddy or grassy greens.

Beyond these spaces
        that vibrate with their energy
and insatiable thirst for motion,
        I, on hard turf,
tiptoe on corners,
        awaiting a wrecking ball
to disrupt the paralysis of my still-life.

On such Sundays,
        from these playgrounds,
the cacophony of children
        goosepimples my skin
and conjures that which
        I must cover again
before placing porcelain palm,
        complete with broken life line,
in pocket and turning away.

Tooth Fairy Supplication

Every third night, or so,
incisors argue over the way to go
in the gummed, gripped dance of
R.E.M.'s fervid stage;

Wrought from engaged wonder,
one waking thought is ever pondered:
> *If it is true, that for every dear person known,*
> *In dreams, a loose tooth represents the fond farewell*
> *Or the bittersweet crown of adieu,*
> *Then can't the gaping mouth make room for*
> *A singular hello,*
> *To silence querying faith,*
> *To placate pulsing fear?*

Tonight, I beckon:

Bring to palate's pillow
> Promise's biting cheer;
Cater to molar memories—
> All mirthful moments seen.
Still grinding jaw provision,
> The painful tongue in cheek,
Until belief fills cavity
> And slippery slopes of sleep.

The Fortune Teller

She welcomes the last client of the day,
      as tiger lily poses in lucent vase,
and candle wax drips aromatics.

Well-composed for the ritual,
      she exhales the habitual
unfolding of plagued woman's divination:

      Shuffle five times, cut, then choose three,
      and we will see
      if hearts or clubs have come to pass.

      Since youth, two accidents occurred,
      but now a faster pace has blurred
      travel ambitions from coming to fruition.

      Your mother hid Holocaust secrets
      once haunting her sleepless
      until the church brought some relief.

      A husband's been buying sleek furs
      for young, eager girls,
      while dinner grows cold at home.

      I see a soulmate on the horizon,
      and the promise of two strong sons or
      even better: a precocious girl.

      Before making hasty depart,
      heed these words: it is smart
      not to ignore the pain on your side.

At reading's close,
      fee is offered from tattered coat pocket
before mystic's cards are folded.

The flame's excise brings smoke and
      invokes a reminder of
the one truth she forgot to tell:

      Beyond all revelations,
         and card face translations,
      Destiny, the King, never outranks
         the Ace of freewill.

At the Stake

I listened to her unburden,
      saw her downcast gaze
      as she revealed to me,
      complete stranger,
      the story of how
      she earned a scarlet letter,
      hidden scar of choice,
      universal taboo.
      Heavy breathed, she took me there:

Outside,
      pore on pore,
      skin-bound and poster-clad
      in slow motion
      they synchronized in parade,
      alone, like rigid trees branching signs,
      together, as missiles spearheaded
      towards a sky and holy trinity
      they claimed was theirs, exclusively.

Inside,
      hands poised up
      clasp-fingered chapel,
      congregations of worry and regret,
      waiting for faith to pull her through and
      make it to the other side.

Outside again,
      chants encircled clinic,
      the collective voice who spoke on behalf
      of a scary god,
      one who hated women
      and preferred the psalms of the many-throated mob,
      wolves in human clothing,
      brazen men,
      celebratory as drunks,
      howling in packs,
      satisfied with those who did not question but followed.
      In Salem, they would have been the first
      to strike the match.

Inside,

> the time was at hand,
> a naked shepherd
> would lose her lamb
> as sterility descended
> and darkness embraced,
> without shadow or light
> in a room with no walls,
> but in every color, a purpose:

White:

> the gloves, the sheets, or doctor's coat,
> and bulbs, the soft feel of
> cotton
> and eyes that did not judge,

Silver:

> Scalpel and stirrups,
> a machine that inhaled stars like a vacuum
> lapping up each sacrifice.

Red:

> Their lips and tongues,
> a pressure that promised to implode
> the stain of blood
> beneath.

Detached and floating,

> she found herself on the outskirts of the Mississippi River,
> though burning still,
> and thirsty for any liquid or living thing
> to bring relief and freedom from guilt,
> she waited for the waters to part,
> convinced she could
> no longer walk on them.

She said it was a time of sinking.

Tryst

By sunrise,
we flush ourselves of weeds,
and soberly
offer final fronds to fire.

Still glowing,
we awkwardly
struggle
to stay silent
as faint blooms of spark
reflect the real combust
of lonely flickers.

In a parallel place,
another dimension,
some similar kindling
will bloom into space,
explode and
consume air;
the virtuous,
sacred
sliver
bond
outpouring of
grace
by two
more connected
and resolved than we

to keep the flame ablaze.

Forced Metamorphosis

An eclipse was promised that night,
in orbit of stars, dreams, and light
to shield girls from what the world emits,
while scorning wishes of the feminine.

She listened as they earnestly endorsed:
If you don't stare straight at the source,
your retinae won't be scorched.
you'll stay safe from sun's remorse—lies!

He waited until the drink went down,
guard was dropped, lids were closed;
post-disco, darkness duped and dosed.
That's when the act came to blows.

Where was Mary, Jesus, Holy Ghost?
Were they also Mickey Finned down the hall,
as their lamb fleeced in the maul
of the hoodwink that would next befall?

She knew the struggle was real
in witness of finger bruises, by morning,
underclothes ripped by a shameless
beast who seized without warning.

The years passed and though that time
seemed long gone and behind
her beau said she was even so inclined
to sleep alone, curled up and crying.

Considering the intruder who once
duped and advanced against will,
she wondered if he was on the streets, still,
or whether another victim scored that kill.

Surviving should have brought relief,
or minimal scar tissue carbon-dated,
as friends, music, and wine sedated
foul thoughts of what was once fated.

But thoughts of wounds, blood, and blue
brought her back to the crisis hotline shrew
whose dead voice once rattled that without DNA
no proof of a crime was there—only injustice, tried and true.

One of Our Best Kept Secrets

You're watching,
and waiting
though the last one left you
arrow-splintered,
cloud-dusted,
God-whipped,
demographically
scattered,
before you were
demoted to me,
woman in need,
lonely and shattered
but still not void of all faith.

Your master has given me signs,
things chance alone can't explain,
like when I won the lotto as hospital bills consumed,
or the night he called and laid on the sugar,
seconds before I was to mail the 'dear john' letter,
jealousy in full bloom.

And, you know,
I've heard of the others,
not all Christ-believing citizens
who have seen theirs,
equal opportunity guardians,
leaving slews of evangelists as their damned.

One day, I'll be worthy of a visit.
Maybe, when I share whiskey shots with
an elusive stranger,
I'll recognize you,
disguised in white silken tweeds,
gold chains falling like haloes
around your neck.

You'll bum a smoke
and ask a string of questions:
      —What do I want to do with the rest of my life?
      —How could I feel so worthless?
and the quintessential

—What is a hot woman like me doing in a place like this?

Defensively, I'll come up with an explanation for the last remark first, like
    —I just got lost in the neighborhood, needed to pee, and got
       thirsty, but, anyway, what the hell is it to you?
And you'll just smile and say, "Whatever".

Then, the bartender,
noticing me talking to an empty stool and
offering cigarettes to air
will call 911 and label me schizophrenic.

I'll know the meaning of cupidity,
when the very institutions from which you tried
to protect will devour in the end.

And you,
depressed over yet another failed mission,
will resort to the streets,
invisible again,
those wings traded for tents and grocery carts,
with sky-ideals that don't quite work on planet Earth,

You,
another homeless angel,
holding up signs
at intersections,
"Will work for food",
secretly cursing Him for never having
taught you the lessons of the
fallen.

Timebombing

You think you don't wear it
on gilded sleeve,
yet you do
live every waking moment
as miserable myth,
pretentious parable.

One lick of the serpent's tongue,
and you burned from
that which took you
two times nine months to become.

Orgy ridden, your body
trickles toxins
that pool in the aftermath
of flesh and soul,
abyss of Earth-time.

Too much liquor melts cubes
in half empty spaces;
glassy-eyed despair fills—
a toast, the spill,
and it's gone until
you distill again with mirrored lines
and millionaire races,
nothing to show for it
but plastic-smiled faces.

A viewer to your film,
I grew voiceless as
thinly-veiled themes exposed
cruel actors sub-plotting
naked, designer labeled dreams,
poorly fashioned,
clearance-saled,
and with each hour:
the price.

Debbie, though I believed
the true, inner victor
wanted all of it

Cut! Take Two!
I realized I couldn't
save you
from the Samurv,
the curse,
yourself or
anything at all
that happened since
the day he stole your children.

Inclemency

Bliss of cirrus wisp,
Cumulonimbus eclipse:
Bowing kiss of rain.

Mimi

On Sunday mornings,
      we woke to light clinks of the prayer string;
as your spotted, once smooth skin
      touched each bead,
with every psalm,
      I wondered how long
      the cross would remain warm in your palm,
that felt like crumpled velvet
      caressing our small faces.

During afternoon's descent,
      little bits of clothed aroma,
flying from your peanut butter soup,
      would beckon us to eat sticky substance;
brother and I forced smiles and chanted,
      "We like it, Grandma"
but spat it out with wrinkled, scrunched mouths
      when your back was turned.

One day, the Phantoms appeared,
You served them chamomile tea and chatted,
answered by voices of the past we could not hear.

They took you away,
      leaving us with dusty remnants:
      —photographs that framed features, frozen at a 20's ball,
      —the lingering, Lily-of-the-Valley smell of you, as if it, too,
      awaited your return,
      —the knitted sweater, left half-completed.

For many tears thereafter,
      we struggled to feel your bedside hymns,
      comforting ones that once escorted us into dreamtime.

For many nights thereafter,
      we convinced ourselves that
      what Mom said were the rings of the porch's wind chimes
      were actually the distant rattlings of your rosary.

Laundromat

There are suds in that washer.

For one dollar and fifty cents I have come to see them.

Through a circle of glass,
window to all those dirty clothes,
I watch their opalescent, shiny spheres
rubbing one against another,
like sticky, small marbles,
snuggling,
or barbie-doll sized crystal balls,
foretelling this load's future.

They are borne of detergent's seeds,
growing then exploding,
while cotton expands and covers,
or polyester absorbs and smothers.
with only seconds to rinse cycle,
they are drowning in hot water,
                choking from the bleach,
                        twisting in the spin.

By the time their memory is haloed in
drain's residue,
they will have become holy suds,
saints of soap,
having redeemed the sins of soil,
having died so pants and shirts
may live.

Collision

There was a time I was sick with rumble,
   thrashing thoughts, ionic tumble,
     altered orbit—stutter, stumble—
       the way a woman, scorned,
   lashes out, aflutter and fumbled,
  while unraveling
and coming undone.
  Our charge of separation,
   cosmic field of instigation,
    wore me thin of heartache, thunder, wind;
     As I, humbled, pondered
      over you—outward, inward,
       under, reaching,
        arching, spanning,
     always seeking spectral clues
  to what went wrong.
Then, a glimpse into the eye,
  when you—shameless, proud, awry—taunted cloud nymphs,
   skirts of sky,
    wink-slinked hints—what potential—
     charming conman with credentials,
      spinning sylphs in sparkling shadows
      glowing wings, complete with arrows:
    silent, blackened, balled or heat,
   ribbon, zigzag, beaded sheet-
  How electric, those lusty needs,
to bring all to sky's frenzied finale and simple bolts ablaze.
   When the calm came,
     I was struck down,
       finally through with a suffering that consumed
      outgrown dreams, old monsoons, weary tears and atmospheres,
    the scatterings of youth's warmth, lies, and fears.
  Oh, that ardent love-storm we shared-
 the way it ravaged and ensnared,
altered, thrashed, rumble-tumbled, grumbled,
 fumbled, stutter-stumbled,
  Yet, here we are, still telling stories,
    post collision, of the scars and incisions
  we wrought while reckless
 and charged
like lightning.

Clarity

This night smells of poetry,
amidst cricket cacophony,
with a climate that quavers
of exhaustion, lust,
and crouched cats with
cutting claws to pounce,
in promise:
prey on the way.

Do you see?
The old, blue moon
that wanes
still waxes on
about
vapors of space,
memory,
and things that might have been—

every one of them
a lesson to be chronicled.

Feel the light that shines through
cracked bedroom door,
so that no one
afraid of the dark
will have to bump into
or bruise from
the corners of words:

sparkling truths
that define the edges of
our shadows.

A graduate of Vassar College and Johns Hopkins University, **Marigo Stathis** is an award-winning executive neuroscientist, consultant, and author, with a plethora of peer-reviewed, technical publications to her credit. With respect to creative writing, poetry has always been her "go to". Since the age of 17, her poems have appeared in various national and international literary journals, magazines and anthologies (e.g., *34th Parallel, Abbey, The Baltimore City Paper, The Baltimore Sun, Bear Creek Haiku, Facedown, FanStory, The Keeping Room, Lite Journal of Satire and Creativity, The Loch Raven Review, The National Library of Poetry, A Question of Balance, The Sometimes,* and *Whispers.* When she isn't conducting research or writing, she can be found with her husband in their Baltimore City garden, harvesting flowers and fruit from wild elderberry shrubs or making healthy concoctions based on the latter. Her latest challenges include learning how to time travel and living a whole day without using expletives (silently or out loud).